# MIRACLES:
# GOD'S CREDIBILITY
## Extraordinary
## Miracles In An
## Ordinary Life

By Dr. Lyn Olsen

This book is dedicated to the God who thought I was worth his love, even when nobody else did.

Through it all, He teaches us how to love and forgive others despite their imperfections and their hate.

PROLOGUE

This book contains a collection of only some of the true extraordinary miracles in one very ordinary life.

Many choose to not believe in God because he does not give them everything they want when they want it nor does he fix the problems that resulted from their bad choices. Is this what God's credibility depends on?

A wise person learns a person cannot know everything, least of all the future. A wise person also learns some things are good for them and some are bad. There are many ways to know what is good for you. Not only does the Bible give us guidance as to what is good and what is not, but there are books written and people who can help us understand what is good and what is bad for us.

Choosing either good or bad can have extreme effects on lives although many who choose bad try to make others suffer the consequences of their bad choices. Unfortunately, no matter how much one tries to justify their bad choices by either making others tell them it is okay or silencing those who disagree with them, sooner or later in one way or other they will be faced with the consequences of their bad choices. That is why we are encouraged to not judge others, because it is by the same we will be judged. A person should tell someone when they think something is a bad choice, especially if the person made the same mistake in their life and changed or if they never did make the bad choice because they knew it was bad. They can tell others when something is bad because either they were already judged if guilty or they never did it because they knew it was bad.

In other words, sometimes God's best answer to prayers is we don't get what we wanted, and I know from experience this is very true. Despite a life of extreme hardships, I persevered in my faith in God and doing good for others. Subsequently I have found a joy and achieved things way beyond anything I ever imagined or hoped for.

Although the Bible says it is wrong of people to demand miracles in order to believe, the disbelief is sad because miracles are everywhere around us, even in our greatly disbelieving and selfish world of today. "Only an evil generation would demand a miraculous sign" in order to believe in God (Matthew 16:4; Luke 11:29; Matthew 12:39; Mark 8:12).

While miracles are all around us, we just don't value them anymore. Instead we desire the things of the world which do not make us happy, but these are a merciless master which make us chase them more and more until it excludes everything else, making it impossible to ever be satisfied, leaving us always wanting more.

While some miracles are visible, the greatest miracles are the ones we can't see but which we treasure the most if we ever receive them. These include real love, forgiveness, and mercy because these gifts are given even though we may not be worthy of them. They are given to us because of the goodness and humbleness of another person and not because we have to be perfect to receive them and despite the bad choices we may make.

Love, forgiveness, and mercy are the greatest miracles because they free us from living a life of bitterness and hate. However, this freedom is dependent on our choosing to not continue to make bad choices and to admit when we are wrong.

My life is a great illustration of how miracles sustained and helped me overcome the worst of circumstances, encouraging me to never succumb to hate and bitterness. That is why I felt compelled to write this book to instill disquietness in those who refuse to believe and courage to continue in faith and love for the believers.

## Chapter 1: MEMORIES AND DREAMS

I don't know if I could even be considered ordinary. Nobody even knew I existed when I was growing up. Other than trudging  miles in bitterly cold winters with forty below temperatures and blizzards dumping several feet of snow, I spent the rest of my time during my junior and high school years cleaning, cooking, laundry and whatever other household duty there was for my siblings as my single mom worked several minimum wage jobs.

My mom was a wonderful and brilliant woman but she lived at a time when women didn't go to college much and so she never was promoted though she was smart and a hard worker, just as her mom had been too. And despite working several jobs, there was never enough food in the house and we had little evidenced by the my wearing the same blue pants and white shirt to school every day.  Thankfully because nobody noticed me, nobody bullied me.

I had no idea where my life was headed for I had no direction from anyone or anywhere. I grew up in a confusing time when there were few good people to encourage or guide others as families were breaking up, both parents worked, and the only other source of information was the valueless media laden with lies, unrealities, distortions, agendas and biases.

Consequently, I rambled through many philosophies and religions, reading every book I could find, searching for answers in our highly dysfunctional world in the hopes of finding my self-worth.  But I found little in the world that cared about who I was on the inside, providing no alleviation for my intense feelings of worthlessness grown from my great loneliness and constant reminders from others of how fat, stupid and ugly I was.

Despite having no idea who I was or where I should go in life, I always sensed God was watching over me, something I would be reminded of many times in my life.  Raised in an ever-increasingly disbelieving culture that taught me to question God and replace him with science, science actually proved again and again to me the existence of God.   It took constant questioning and many years of searching for me to stop questioning and arguing with God, and listen instead.

One of the most important lessons I learned through all of this wandering and confusion was his plans for me were far greater than the plans I had for myself.  He certainly saw more good in me than I or anybody else did.  In truth, while the world emphasized my worthlessness, God never gave up on me.

As young as four-years-old, my memories and dreams were the beginning of my closeness to God and his miracles in my life though I didn't really comprehend it then. I remember my memories and dreams as whole scenes, like watching a show with great detail and action throughout. Some of my dreams and nightmares I dreamed over and over and remember even to this day. They were oftentimes long and complicated as well as very active including my walking and talking in my sleep. I remember several times cleaning the house when I was in grade school while sound asleep. Later when I woke up, still remembering my dream, I would see the cleaning supplies on the table where I left them in my dream.

My earliest memories and dreams go back to around age four when we lived on Rodney Street in Helena, Montana. One of my most prominent nightmares involved the two lions who sat up high on a hill overlooking the steps that wound down from the huge stone house on the hill. "They are going to eat me!" I feared every time I walked past them for I truly feared they would come alive. I feared them so much, sure they would come to life in my four-year-old mind, that I would cross the street to walk on the other side away from them, fairly confident that I would then have enough time to run if they sprang to life.

Every weekend my Auntie Alice miraculously would drive from Butte to Helena in her little convertible VW bug to spend time with us. I say miraculously because the road between Helena and Butte was one lane in each direction over steep mountain passes that wound back and forth and up and down. Oftentimes these roads were closed and impassable with several feet of snow dumped by huge blizzard yet still my Auntie drove back and forth to see us every weekend.

Because she had the first convertible VW bug in Butte, every Christmas she drove Santa to town through the streets of uptown Butte. We all loved the bug because she would put the convertible top down and we would sit on top of it, flying down the street. There were no seatbelts back then and sometimes it is surprising we survived our childhoods. I, though, did not get to ever sit up there though I desperately wanted to grow up and be able to, but Auntie Alice said I was too young. She drove that car forever, even until the floorboards began to rust out.

We didn't have much in those days, so treats were rare. But every Sunday morning my Auntie Alice walked us kids down to the penny candy store. This was the most anticipated day of our little lives in those days for it was our only candy. She gave us each ten cents but making decisions regarding which ten pieces of candy I wanted seemed incredibly hard as a four-year-old. This was especially true for the huge glass display case towered over me and was filled with every kind of penny candy. Patiently my Auntie asked over and over, "Have you decided yet?" "Um, um," I mumbled over and over despite her constant reminder to hurry up for I never found it easy to decide despite having though all week about which ten pieces of candy I would pick the next Sunday.

"Oh, how I wish I could go to school!" I thought as I stood in front of the school my brothers went to. "How lucky they are!" I was sure then that I would never get the chance to go to school because I wanted so very much to go. I can still see the school and remember standing in front of it as though I was there right now. Sadly I thought that I would never get to go to school when I learned we were moving. Happily I learned afterwards there were other schools in town.

Despite being the worst student in the beginning of school, I still loved school at Broadwater Elementary School. I can still see the inside of the school and my classrooms. I remember and loved the smells of the school and its cleaning supplies, chalk boards, and books. I also remember the outside, especially the May Pole around which we children gathered every spring as it was quite charming, though I never really knew why we gathered around the pole though I always did as I was told.

I started out as the worst student for one reason. In first grade, perhaps because my last name begin with a letter at the end of the alphabet, I always sat at the back of the classroom. I still remember vividly the day my teacher moved students around and moved me to the front of the class. It was incredible! I could see words and letters on the chalk board! As a small child I had no idea that I was missing out on this and had no idea that not being able to see what was on the chalk board was the reason I never did well in school. I was so excited to see the letters and words, but sadly, just as quickly she moved me to the back of the room again. Because I never did well in first grade, I was the only student who never got the Friday treat which was kool-aid. Again, we didn't get many treats back then so this was a huge deal, especially since I never got any.

It was not until the end of second grade when they tested all of the students for vision that they discovered I needed glasses. Thankfully, my third grade teacher, Ms. Chamberlin (teachers weren't allowed to marry back then), did not label me as a bad and hopeless student as some teachers may do. Instead, she would pull me aside, stand me in front of her metal carousel full of her books, and tell me, "I know you are smart. I know you can read all of my books. And if you do, then I will introduce you to Ms. Potter, the fourth grade teacher, so you can read her books too!"

With her encouragement, I did read all of her books and became one of the best students in her class and overcoming all challenges became a lifelong pattern. In fact, forever after I was always the best student in my classes and reading became my source of hope and my means of escape when life got too tough.

My memories of Helena are filled with vivid details of the streets and houses in my neighborhood. I remember many of the homes including the one on the corner opposite our grade school. I remember it well because it was Charlie Pride, the country-western singer's, home. He lived there with his wife and daughter and in first grade I went to his daughter's birthday party. This birthday was memorable because they took all of us kids to the movies which nobody ever did because nobody had the money to go even though it cost less than a dollar.

Our neighborhood was an older neighborhood with some very dilapidated and downright scary houses. Their scariness was exacerbated by the horror stories told by my brothers and friends. My friend lived behind our house in the only apartment house in our neighborhood which was very old, dark and creepy, especially after her horrible stories of people who had been murdered there. With the advent of horror movies in those days, many featuring Vincent Price, it didn't take much to put the fear in a small child.

And I lived with that fear in many ways. Especially the house next to my friend's house behind us. It was straight out of a horror story, a Bates mansion kind of house. It was a dark and forbidding house. Old rotting wood and broken bricks were the bones of the house outlined by over-grown weeds and windows so dirty no light could get in or out. No one had ever seen anyone come out, nor anyone coming back out. We dared each other constantly to run up to the house and not get caught, always hoping someone might so we could either confirm our greatest fear or eliminate it when they did safely return but nobody ever took the dare.

Walking back and forth from Broadwater School, I remember the crisp yellow, orange and brown autumn leaves which I strived to make as much noise as I could when I jumped on them, inhaling their sweet fragrance when crushed. Along with the autumn leaves also came the deepening dark evenings as night came earlier and earlier, signaling the harsh, bitterly cold winter was near. The bitter cold presented many challenges including the frozen tongue dare. Kids were always challenging each other to stick their tongue on the frozen metal monkey bars or merry-go-rounds. Enjoying a challenge, I contemplated it but knew too well the other stories of what happened when a tongue was stuck to the metal, having to be ripped off.

Our house was a brick two story with my room on the second floor. My brothers all shared a room which my father began remodeling but never finished.

I remember every intricate detail of every room of our house on Peosta. I remember being devastated when I burned a waffle shape on my new coat when it fell on the floor furnace. I remember the bookshelf standing behind my mother as she ironed which consumed a lot of her time back then as everything was ironed using a glass pop bottle with an attachment on the top that allowed water to sprinkle out. Two books on the bookshelf behind her that intrigued me greatly were "Why Johnny Can't Read" and another with a beautiful woman on the front whose one hand was raised with her lovely fingers touching each other.

"Splat" was the sound my brother's face made when it hit the concrete sidewalk.  Many kinds of fruits and vegetables grew wild in Helena as well as most people having gardens. Gardens though were well guarded, just like in the Tale of Peter Rabbit. Rarely did we have enough courage to rob the gardens, so very afraid we would be caught.  Berries, rhubarb, onions, and crab apples were plentiful everywhere. Though sour and small, we still thought it was worth the effort to climb the large trees and steal the small apples.   It was from the tree in our own yard that overlooked the concrete sidewalk that my brother fell out and landed face first.

Though their smell sweetly filled the air, I never liked the taste of the wild onions that grew across the street in the back alley which bordered on the graveyard filled with old, weathered, concrete headstones.  It was a fearsome cemetery, especially for someone so young, and it was also where my monsters in my nightmares came from, monsters who were always looking for children.  Every time my nightmares with their monster came, I contemplated for a long time how to escape the monster, always ending up hiding in the kitchen cupboards.

My nightmares had other sources besides the cemetery. One night I had watched a scary movie, "The Crawling Hand," on TV as scary movies became popular in the early 1960s. My room in our house on Peosta was an unusual shaped room on the second floor of our old brick house with the bed centered in the middle, facing the only door into the room. It was through this one doorway the hand came crawling for me.

"I know it's going to kill me," I said to myself over and over, building up my fear worse than it had to be and limiting my courage to make a run for it. With the blankets pulled tight over my entire body, and especially my head, I debated what my better chances of surviving were. "Would pulling the blankets up tight around me keep it from seeing me and killing me?" or "Would running past it to my parents' room be my only hope?"

It seemed forever as the hand kept crawling closer and closer to me for somehow it kept crawling but never got nearer, but rather it continued to block the only doorway and means of escape. I contemplated for a long time what my chances were of running past without it grabbing my leg, taking me down and killing me. "Go, go!" I kept echoing to myself, trying to gather the courage to make the run, knowing sooner rather than later it would eventually get to me. Finally and bravely, I mustered enough courage and sprinted from the bed, past the crawling hand and flew down the stairs to my parents' room. "What great luck," I thought. It didn't get me though I didn't know how as I was a little girl and it was so big, standing in the only doorway to my room.

"Go back to your room!" my parents responded when I finally found the safety of their room. I stood in disbelief. "They couldn't really mean I should back to the crawling hand which waited to kill me," I thought. As I stood there, sure they couldn't have meant that, they ordered me again to return to my room. Years later I surmised that it must have been a Dr. Spock thing where my parents were not allowed to protect me from the monsters upstairs in my room.

"Wake up!" my mom called over and over. I always loved to sleep in late, so waking up at 6 am was something I never enjoyed in my life, especially as a small child. But this one day was the exception. I was excited and had been waiting for her to wake me for it was Thanksgiving and the turkey had be put in if ever we were going to eat on time. Growing up in snow-ridden, subzero Montana, this day was one of my best and most vivid memories. As we prepared the stuffing and turkey, the windows would steam up through which the snow falling could be seen all day for it always snowed on Thanksgiving Day in Montana. It was terribly comforting to know I would not have to go outside into the freezing cold but rather could stay inside the warmth of the kitchen filled with the unforgettable aroma of the turkey cooking, then later stuff ourselves with the most delicious food for my mom was a great cook. Every detail of those days remain vivid in my memories, allowing me to dream of them as though they just happened, allowing me to relive those days as though they just happened.

From the wading pool at the Civic Center with its lone skinny tower to the bum's jungle where the homeless lived next to the train tracks, I remember our many adventures in Helena as a child. The bum's jungle and the train tracks ran under the street bridge which was the only way to the rest of the city and the park. It was a very narrow dirt uneven path that was oftentimes covered with ice and snow. Every time I braved crossing it to keep up with my brothers so I wouldn't miss out on their fun but I always feared slipping far down to my death. I wasn't sure what a bum's jungle was but feared it all.

I remember many scenes from my childhood as though they were being acted out again. "She will be president," Bobby argued with his brother as we all stood in front of the porch of our house. "No," his brother yelled back. "Her brother will be president!" Not sure why this was an important argument but I can still see my two young neighbors fighting and the intensity with which the youngest boy, Bobby, defended me. We were the best of friends. I have many memories of him including seeing us coloring on his front porch.

Chapter 2: QUAKES AND LAKES

Miracles are all around us, we just can't see them, or don't want
to see them because then we would have to believe in their
creator. Sometimes they are obvious, sometimes a part of our
everyday life, and sometimes happening against all odds. In my
life there are examples of all kinds. An apt analogy to faith in
the Creator is the acknowledgement that a watch needs a
beginning and an intelligent designer. Yet disbelievers don't
think the most complex creation, ourselves, needed an
intelligent designer but instead was a series of misadventures
and random acts. We are such an incredible creation that even
the slightest alteration in our makeup would make everything
nonfunctional and non-existent.

Growing up in the 1950's and 60's we never had much and we
never got to go anywhere. In those days people didn't go on

vacations often, and when they did it usually wasn't far from home. Airplanes weren't common nor were cars with families fortunate to have only one car. There were no malls, few restaurants, no fast food and no money. So when my Auntie Alice would take us on a trip it was a momentous occasion and a lifelong memory.

Most of our trips were in western Montana where we lived, but if you have ever been to western Montana you know you couldn't ask for more beautiful. We never grew tired of traveling the state and the outdoors was five minutes out of any town. Rivers and lakes are nestled at the bottom of the immense Rocky Mountains whose peaks were capped most of the year with snow. The bottoms of the rivers and lake were so clear that everything, including shimmering rocks and flitting fish, were visible. In the evenings, the moonlight would reflect off the rivers and lakes, illuminating clouds brushing across it, creating ever-changing scenes showing the beauty of God's great mountainous creations. This beauty was confirmed by Charles Kuralt who wrote in his journeys across America that the most beautiful place was the Beartooth Mountains in southern Montana. I agree wholeheartedly but to experience this you have to have enough heart to drive its windy narrow road rising and winding back and forth thousands of miles upward out of Red Lodge into the Yellowstone Park area.

"Yipee!" Kevin exclaimed. It was going to be a great day for he and my two older brothers were going on a camping trip with Auntie Alice to Yellowstone Park. "What do I pack?" Kevin had no idea what to pack because this was his first trip. He watched his brothers to figure it out because they were older and smarter after all, ranging in age from 6 to 10. They packed a few clothes as suggested by Auntie Alice which included short and long sleeve shirts, pants and shorts as you never knew in

Montana what the weather might be, even in the middle of summer when it could snow.

Packed and ready to go, the three boys sat on the porch, waiting for Auntie Alice to drive up. It was only going to be a couple of days over the weekend as most vacations were with her. During the week she worked as the advertising manager for Hennessy's department store. She created all of the ads including the artwork, then submitted her work to the local newspaper which used typesetting, a rather tedious time-consuming task requiring laying out of each letter and picture. She was extremely dedicated to work and so our trips with her were wedged in between her job duties. Because of this, the trip would usually start later than she originally planned. Oftentimes she would tell us we would leave Thursday night, but then she didn't get home until late from work. "Tomorrow, bright and early," she would explain. "But I have just a couple of small things I can do quick in the morning and then away we go." Sometimes the trips began as late as Saturday morning.

There they sat, and sat, staring down the road, switching their stare from side to side in case she came a different way. "The next car is hers!" is the game they would play to see who would be first to say it when it was her. After awhile they tired of it, and waited patiently.

From inside the window, I watched forlornly. How desperately I wanted to go, but everyone ignored my pouting and sighs. Too young they said. I wondered if I would ever grow up in these times. I wondered when would I ever get a chance or would I always be forgotten and left behind for my young life existed day by day, sometimes moment by moment, and I understood little about what the future was.

Inside I watched every tick tock of the clock which gave the feeling that time stood still and she would never come. I could hear my brothers' moans intensifying with doubt encroaching into and quieting their former elation. "Is she here yet?" Every once in a while Kevin moaned, drawing each syllable out slowly as though it might last until she was there. He had asked this question too many times and it had begun to irritate the other two brothers who were now easily annoyed. At our young age, time was greatly valued as none of us had become bored with life yet. It was also valued because trips were rare so every moment lost mattered. "No," Eric mumbled grumpily, ready to strangle Kevin if he asked one more time.

Everything changes in life, though, and soon the putter of her VW could be heard as it rounded the corner. Having waited so long and stored up so much anticipated energy, they piled into the VW quickly, hoping it would prevent any further delays such as Auntie Alice having to talk to someone else or do something else. She was ready though and loaded with treats we never had otherwise. She also brought along her 1950's brownie video camera, a rare item to have then, which would give us glimpses many years later into our earliest years.

It was August 17, 1959. They headed south to Yellowstone Park, a place we visited many more times in our lives. We never tired of seeing and camping in Yellowstone Park, certainly a unique and incredible place. After a short time, as kids are apt to do because of their lack of any concept of time, Kevin began asking, "Are we there yet?" Over and over he asked til Eric slugged him in the arm. "Shut up, I told you!" he yelled. Being younger and smaller, Kevin knew better than to push it, quieting down quickly but still his built-up energy was evidenced in the twitching of his legs with his head stuck out the window for air conditioning in Montana back then consisted of rolling all of the windows down.

As they passed the first lake, all three boys screeched, "Can we stop? Can we stop?"  Lakes meant swimming and lots of other fun.  When traveling in Montana, its great beauty evokes the desire to stop at every lake and river.  Having left late, the boys were full of energy but also hungry so they piled out of the car, toting the picnic basket behind them.  The basket was full of bologna sandwiches, chips and even soda, treats they otherwise never had.  Despite it being August, the lake was cool as many are in Montana but it didn't thwart the boys at all for what seemed cold to most other people seemed perfect to Montanans.  With mouths still stuffed and shorts substituting for swimming trunks, they jumped into the water, seeing who could make the biggest splash.

They continued on to other lakes and rivers, ending up at Madison Canyon by Hebgen Lake on the way out of the park. They were exhausted from swimming and playing and the fresh outdoor air, so they quickly gulped down hot dogs cooked over a wood fire they had made from collecting sticks.  "Somehow," they all thought as they finished up, "everything always tasted better cooked over a camp fire."  With the rhythm of the river lulling them to sleep, they snuggled in for the night in their campground.

Unexpectedly and suddenly, Auntie Alice who loved her sleep as much as anyone, jumped up.  "Let's go!  Grab everything." she exclaimed.  The boys weren't sure if she was serious or not, but they went along with it, helping her pack up everything.

It was so strange for her to do this. Auntie Alice was a decisive person who planned carefully, so she never changed her plans.

She was also a person who enjoyed her rest and relaxation, especially beside a river.  It was only that night she decided at this late hour to leave, so out of the park into the Ennis area they drove.

At 11:37 that night a major 7.8 earthquake hit, dropping the entire mountainside down into the lake and damning the river, killing everyone near within moments which would have been my aunt and brothers.  "The landslides caused by the quake carried 80 million tons (40 million cubic yards) of rock, mud and debris down into the valley and created hurricane-force winds strong enough to toss cars. In Madison Canyon, the landslide swept away a family of seven, five of whom perished. In Rock Creek, tourists camping there were caught off guard by the quake and landslide, which swept them into the creek" (Wikipedia.com).

Shortly after that another miraculous and unexpected event saved my family.  'NO!" my mom exclaimed.  She was adamant this one and only time.  My father had been drinking as he had come to do most of the time. Sadly, I have few memories of him when he was not drunk.

Although Auntie Alice usually came over every weekend faithfully to see us in Helena, on rare occasions we drove to Butte to see my mom's family. This particular day had been one of those days.  My mother's family get-togethers were always brimful with the best of every kind of food imaginable as my Aunties, my mom, and especially my grandmother were some of the best cooks around.  In fact, my grandmother was a perfectionist in everything she did, and in particular with food. None of us children have few memories of our grandmother that did not include the finest epicurean foods perfected by her in her laboratorial kitchen for she spent many hours to ensure her food was the best.

This weekend was no different, and stuffed with having over-eaten because the food was too good to stop eating, my father likewise had drank too much. He was highly intoxicated and belligerently demanding, a way of life that I would live with until my parents divorced many years later.

"YOU WILL GO HOME WITH ME!" he shouted at my mother. Too drunk to care much what others thought, he was more angry that she was refusing to go home with him because he thought he should be the only one in control.

As hard and frightening as it was to say "no", she didn't want to say it again, so she ignored him. This was tough for her as my mom was a very quiet, good-natured, kind person who never liked yelling and screaming fights. Throughout her entire life she never liked confrontations and she preferred to give in and suffer than to further antagonize the situation. Unfortunately, this nature did not serve her well as she was never appreciated by the men in her life as she should have been although all of us kids did appreciate her and loved her dearly. Rightfully so though because she sacrificed everything for us and worked day and night at minimum wage jobs to put a roof over our head and meager food on our table though we never had enough money to buy or do anything else.

Ignoring him though only seemed to make my dad angrier. My dad continued yelling at her. In his drunken rage, he screamed again and again, "YOUR ARE GOING WITH ME, ALL OF YOU. I WON'T LEAVE WITHOUT YOU." "I won't," she said determinedly with her head bowed down, afraid to look into his face, ashamed and fearful.

"Well, the kids are coming then with me then!" he bellowed, hoping that this would sway her to come with him.

Again, for the only time in her life with my dad she plainly stated, "No, they are not." It only infuriated him even more when she petulantly added, "You are too drunk. They won't be going with you either, none of us."

In those days drinking was glorified in hollywood and the culture as well as smoking and was a significant part of sociality. People never worried about the consequences of driving drunk, everyone did it. There were no repercussions either, at least legally. People never considered it wrong to drive drunk nor did the people who rode with them.

Although my mom tried hard for many years to please my father in all ways, this one time, the only time, my mom would not give in to her husband's demands. As she stood there, trembling but not moving despite his continuing onslaught against her, he finally burst out of my grandmother's house and sped off into the dark night, tires squealing, heading back to Helena alone.

The color drained out of her face and weak from her battle, my mom could not fall asleep. After all of us kids were tucked into bed at her sister's house, she sat at the kitchen table, wondering what repercussions she would face when she saw him again for he could be violent and abusive, especially when drunk and he was almost always drunk.

The repercussions never came. Later that night she received a phone call from the sheriff. Shortly after leaving Butte my dad had driven off the cliff by Elk Park and plunged several hundred feet down the steep embankment, landing upside down in the lake at the bottom. Being drunk, he survived but, the sheriff affirmed unequivocally that if we had been in the car none of us would have survived.

In the many trips I have since taken between Helena and Butte, I always think about how different everything would have been if my family and I no longer existed.

## CHAPTER 3 ALL'S FAIR

The World's Fair in the early to mid-1900's was the grandest of all events. Those who got to attend were the few and fortunate because it was far away and nobody had the money to travel that far. The rest of us consoled ourselves with small traveling carnivals that came to our towns once a year. My family did not have the money to take a long trip as most was spent on booze. As much as I dreamed of going to the World's Fair in New York City I knew it was impossible.

My family never went to church though sometimes as a small child I would ask to be dropped off at the church in town though not sure why. So, silly as it seems in my childish ways, I prayed incessantly for this impossibility of going to the World's Fair. Being in third grade at that time, I would lie in my bed and pray to God to be able to go to the World's Fair. Faithfully every night I would finish my prayer with "and dear God I want to go to the World's Fair."

Night after night passed and I prayed constantly. Then one night my father came in and sat down on my bed, something he didn't do often and said, "I have to tell you something Lyn." I had absolutely no idea what he would say.

"We are moving to New York. I have a new position there with the phone company as their engineer," he told me.

Without hesitation, I exclaimed, "Then we can go to the World's Fair?!"

"Yes," he promised. I knew it was the answer to my prayer. And we did go to the World's Fair. I'll never forget the Belgium waffles and seeing "It's a Small World" with the World's Fair being its first debut in 1964, later becoming a ride at Disneyland in 1966. And I will never forget the horror of my brother getting lost there. He said he wasn't lost, but we just couldn't find him. It brought an abrupt end to our day at the World's Fair.

Later, after many years of trying had to make the marriage work, my mom filed for divorce and moved us all back to Montana to be near her family so she could get help raising us kids. I'll never forget watching my dad standing at the Kennedy airport in New York City as we boarded the plane to leave him behind. I'll never forget the tears I saw on his face for he had been unable to defeat the monster that was slowly taking away everything good that he loved the most in his life, which was us.

All of these changes left me very lonely during my junior and high school years. While others were going out with their friends, I spent all my time cleaning the house, doing dishes, laundry, cooking and shopping with only $25 a week for food for all of us kids. There was never any money to do anything, something we kids were used to so we never asked our mother for anything because we knew it would make her sad that she couldn't buy anything for us despite being constantly gone for she worked several minimum wage jobs. I remember still my great joy when my mom gave me her own clothes as hand-me-downs which replaced my one white shirt and blue pants that I wore every day to school.

The only solace I could find from all of my pain and poverty were long lonely walks at all hours of the day and night, even when it was bitterly cold below zero weather or blizzards that obscured everything. I had no one to comfort me, to talk to me.

No one at school knew me either and no teacher or counselor ever talked to me. I thought this was a good thing because at least I was not in trouble. That is why it was a surprise in my senior year when I was called to the counselor's office.

I had no idea why the counselor would be calling me to their office. I began to overly obsess what I must have done wrong for there had been many moments in my life, and there would be many more, when I would be blamed for something I never did. In those days we students feared getting in trouble because our parents and school administrators did not tolerate students misbehaving.

There I sat in the counselor's office, anxiously waiting and wondering. "Ms. Olsen, can you come in please?" the counselor asked.

Nervous, I was surprised at how pleasant the counselor was and began to hope that I was not in trouble. "How's it going?" she asked me. "Good," I replied.

"That's good," and she dismissed me. That was the most attention I had ever gotten from any school official throughout all of my high school years. No one ever talked to me or encouraged me to think about what I was going to do after high school, especially about college despite, as I learned many years later, I my being one of the top students in my school.

Poor and unknowing, I never thought about college because neither I nor my mother could ever afford it; we could barely put food on the table. I felt fortunate when I got a part-time job working at a fabric store and started earning money to buy clothes and other things I never could before, but I knew it would never be enough to go to college. I didn't give college another thought.

"Please call me so we can arrange a meeting as soon as possible," began the annoying phone messages from the counselor at the small college in my small town. So I ignored him because I wasn't going to college, I had no money.

But he continued calling over and over. Finally, tired of his unrelenting phone calls, I finally conceded to meet with him.

"I need you to fill out these forms," he said. "That I can do," I thought, filling them out, thinking I was rid of him forever.

To my great dismay some weeks later, he began calling again. "Ms. Olsen, can you meet with me as soon as possible." I had already learned previously that he would not go away, so off I trudged to meet him, dismayed that my previous efforts to avoid him had failed.

"We have a tuition waiver, scholarships, a federal pell grant and some other monies for you to go to college. You will be able to go to college for free as well as getting extra money for other things like books," he explained. Though shocked and unsure what was happening, I didn't hesitate to accept.

I did indeed go to college and earned my bachelor's degree, and later several graduate degrees. I later discovered that my high school ranking was 5 out of 550 student, something nobody had ever told me. Since then I have been able to help thousands and thousands of other people of all ages and circumstances, even the homeless, abused, disabled, and poor go to college and subsequently get great jobs, changing their whole lives as dramatically as the counselor had once changed mine.

## CHAPTER 4 TRIPS NEAR AND FAR

Young adults are oftentimes overly concerned with themselves and I certainly was. I think much of my self-centeredness was because of the loneliness and worthlessness I had felt growing up as a teenager due to my difficult family situation and poverty. My world began to change drastically in my senior year of high school after I got a job and actually had money to buy clothes and take better care of myself. It continued to change in college because I began to discover that there were people who liked me, so I began going out all the time. Being consumed now if others liked me, I never really thought about the presence of God in my life despite his continuing to watch over me and even perform miracles in my life. There are many incidences which I am not sure I would have survived if God had not been watching over me.

Part of my college experience that I had never imagined was the opportunity to study abroad in France. What an indescribable sense of horror and fright when I landed in Paris and discovered that the people all spoke French! I had no idea of how to find the right bus to the designated hotel or even how to find a bathroom.

Living in a small town in Montana at a time when people tried to be nice, I was very naïve and unaware of bad things that could happen. I had taken several college courses in languages including French, but nothing could have prepared me for the shock of being a stranger in a land where I couldn't communicate and where I had no idea what was going on.

The bus I was supposed to take from the airport had been cancelled, so I wondered if I would be stuck at the airport or if I would ever find my way to the city. This was a time where the only directions could be found on a paper map but I had never ridden a train or subway before so I understood nothing on the maps, and I couldn't understand anything anyone said.

Lost and confused, ever appearing the epitome of a vulnerable tourist, I began toting my big suitcase through the subway system, jumping on one train after another, back and forth and around and around with no idea where I was going.

It was a Sunday, my birthday actually. Perhaps because it was Sunday it wasn't terribly busy. On the other hand there was less hope of finding someone to help me find my way who would be willing to speak English.

There I sat on the subway trains, feeling destitute and hopeless, with my huge luggage next to me when a gang of older boys jumped on just before the doors closed. So there I sat alone, and despite the car being completely empty, they had to sit right in front of me where they could stare at me. Though I didn't know much, I knew this was not good.

They began yelling and talking to me, but I had no idea what they were saying. Still they all continued to stare at me. If they were hoping for a verbal response it certainly was not coming from me. All I could think to do is pray for I had no one to help me.

On we traveled. Still they stared, their comments never ceasing.

For what seemed forever, the train finally stopped and I picked up my suitcase, wondering what would happen now, and I stepped off the train. They watched as I exited, and the door shut behind me. I wonder still today how many times we don't know when God is watching.

When younger, we were so used to below zero weather and blizzards dumping several feet of snow that we never worried about the blizzards, driving through anything. Blizzards were a constant way of life in Montana though so we learned to survive and drive any kind of weather. In the 1970's some of the Montanan roads were still one lane in each direction winding through steep mountain passes oftentimes coated with black ice and heaping snow. Winds over 80 mph oftentimes created blinding white snow, reducing visibility to nothing, sometimes even sliding cars off the icy roads. Grace was a sanding truck or plow whose path you followed closely.

Despite bad weather, driving in Montana was never boring but instead incredibly gorgeous. While in college, oftentimes in the middle of the night, I would take off in my old VW bug, flying down the highways, reveling in the glow of the moon off the rivers as it peeked over the mountaintops.

Though my VW was old, it always worked despite my trying several times mistakenly to kill it. It certainly was the reliable car the Germans built it to be. If the battery was dead or the starter gone, I would park the car on a hill and as it began to roll I would pop the clutch and it would start.

Part of the reliability of the car was due to how basic it was as evidenced by the small engine at the back of the car that provided no heat within the car. In the bitterly cold winters when everything was frozen in ice with temperatures below zero, I would have to stop repeatedly on the highway and scrape the windows as ice formed quickly over it.

Sometimes I got lucky though when driving home and got to drive one of my mom's Avis-Rent-A-Car back home from Missoula or other places for these were luxury cars compared to my old VW, though I never complained about my VW.  It was in the dead of winter one late afternoon when my sister and I were driving one of her cars back to Butte from Missoula.  It was a dark grey day because the snow clouds hung low, hugging the ground, reducing visibility to almost nothing.  But that didn't stop us as it never did in our younger days.

Sometimes in those days you never knew how bad the road was ahead because communication was limited and there was no internet, not even phones, where you could check the weather and roads ahead.  Little did we know as we headed out that day onto the highway that it was closed shortly after we got on it due to a major blizzard.

What should have been a two-hour trip turned into hours and hours as we drove at half the speed limit, skating slowly down icy roads hidden by blowing and deepening snow with few highway markers or lights for guidance.  When finally, we could see the mountains of Butte ahead of us as we ascended one of the last hills, we both sighed for we knew we would make it safely to Butte.

 "Whew," Becky exclaimed, as we relaxed and I loosened my grip on the steering wheel, grinning from ear to ear for it was a great relief to know the trip was over.  The snow seemed to have lightened too though the darkness remained.  Reassuringly I added, "Almost there now."  The road ahead of us appeared clear and easy.

Moments later, we both stared in disbelief.  In front of us underneath an overpass was a car jack-knifed in the highway.  Though only moments away from us, I didn't panic for not only was I driving slow, but this was highway had two lanes in each direction.

"No problem," I reassured my sister.  "I'll just pull to the other lane and slide around."

Sliding confidently to the left, staring straight ahead, Becky's screams jolted me.

"A boat, a boat!" she yelled.

Unsure what she meant, I turned towards her to see a huge boat looming over us, completely blocking the only other lane!  We stared in total disbelief because nobody pulls a boat in Montana in the middle of a winter blizzard.

Not thinking at all but turning the steering wheel and pumping the brakes haphazardly, I waited for the crunching sound of us colliding together. But no sound came.

As we reached within a foot of the boat, our car turned sidewise, paralleling the boat, slid forward, and then at just the right moment straightened out at the end of the boat and sailed around it without even a slightest touch.

We were both stunned, saying nothing but breathing hard. "I could have touched that boat, we were so close," my sister finally muttered.

So absorbed in the intensity of the moment, when I looked into my rear view mirror, I was surprised to see several cars right behind me, leaving me to wonder how we didn't collide with any of them too.

There were moments in my life that defied any concept of coincidences, begging for acknowledgement of a creator who loves each one of us. On one fine day in late spring on a beautiful warm day in Montana I did something I had never done before and would never do again. I skipped school and work and drove the couple hour trip to see my mom and Auntie Alice. I am from a generation that was taught the work ethic so I never missed school and I never missed work, except for this one time.

I hoped that I would be able to get there in time for lunch as my Auntie Alice was always generous to us kids. And she did not let me down. Because of its great variety of ethnic cultures, Butte has great food. One place to get great food in 1970s was Terri's. Terri's was a local restaurant on Harrison in Butte where we had gone many times before, and our particular favorite was the Butte pastie, unequalled anywhere.

For some unknown reason, Terri's had moved their tables very close to each other, something they had never done before and would never do again. While totally immersed in the deliciousness of my pastie interspersed with brief comments to my Auntie, suddenly we both heard the guys next to us say the name "Myrna."

"Myrna" is my mom's name. Butte is not a big town and Myrna is not a common name, so we both stopped talking and listened which was easy since we were close enough to be sitting at their table. Several more times her name fluttered out in their conversation, and then they mentioned "Milo," who is my stepfather, another unusual name. So, we knew they were talking about my mom.

Milo, my stepdad had begun his own business owning a small gas station when he was younger in uptown Butte by the Hennessy building. My mom had worked at an insurance company at the Capri Motel half a block away so she would take her car into his service station which is where they met. Later, Milo grew his business into several large companies including owning Avis Rent-A-Car and a huge diesel wrecker and repair yard. He was well known as a shrewd and highly amiable respectable business man who everyone admired. You could find him most every morning at the 4B's café, having breakfast with someone because everyone loved being around him. He was a big man, not so much tall, as wide and solid. Stories told of him was he could outwork anyone, even young men half his age. When Milo and my mom got married she helped him grow his businesses and became manager of Avis Rent-A-Car which was highly successful under her management.

During the same time period as our lunch, Milo had decided to sell his service station and the Avis Rent-A-Car franchise to one of the men sitting next to us with one caveat being that he would keep my mom on as manager. As we listened, we heard the man say, "When I get done here, I am going up to sign the deal with Milo. And as soon as the deal is signed, Myrna is out though I had promised Milo I would keep her as manager."

I doubt you need to be told the rest of the story. "Hello mom. Guess what?" my Auntie and I told my mom. When the man came up to sign the contract for the deal, Milo exclaimed in colorful terms, "You dumb SOB. There is no deal. Her sister and daughter were sitting right next to you at lunch when you told of how you would fire Myrna!"

This was one of those most valuable life lessons we should all learn. Never say anything about others you don't want them to hear because one way or another they will know what you said, sometimes in the most bizarre circumstances.

## CHAPTER 5 BITES AND STINGS

There are many ways God can touch our lives, and dreams are one way. My dreams have always been dramatic and memorable. One night, a couple of nights before visiting my mom two hours away in Butte, I had a nightmare that repeated itself over and over again so that when I work in the morning I remembered every detail of it and still remember to this day.

My mom and stepdad owned a Hoytt Doberman trained to kill anyone. The only two people he liked were my mom and stepdad; that did not include us kids. He was trained as a guard dog and most often was with my stepdad at his wrecker yard, only coming home later in the evening.

Whenever we would visit my mom, we had to worry he might attack us, as it pretty much would have been over for us being the trained killer that he was. I remember late nights when my brother, sister and I would sneak into the house, tiptoeing, hoping the flimsy gate by my mom's bedroom that lay between him and us was not only shut but strong enough so he couldn't get through. There had already been a few instances when it wasn't, and while he flew fast and furious at us, we flew even faster, diving into our bedrooms and slamming the doors shut behind us.

Perhaps it was not unusual then that my nightmare that night several days before I visited my mom centered on the dog. I kept dreaming over and over that he attacked me at my mom's house. Each time I dreamed it I kept trying to figure out a way to save myself.

With the dream still fresh in my memory, when I visited my mom several days later, I kept thinking about it. I even asked my mom if my stepdad and his dog would be coming home early but she adamantly said no. It was Saturday so my stepdad and his dog would not be home until much later as Saturday was a busy day.

I spent the morning helping my mom clean her trailer. It was still early, around noon, when my mom asked me, "Can you put my clean clothes in my bedroom."

"Sure," I said. This meant that I had to walk into her room, the room where the dog spent his life when home.

As I deposited the clothes in her bedroom, I hesitated. My dream remained vivid in my mind and foremost in my memory.

When I reached her door, I stopped to listen though there were no sounds. I stood there with my hand on the door, and waited.

In a few seconds I heard the back door open that led from the outside of the house to their bedroom down a very short hallway. At the same time I heard the bounding thumps of a huge dog running fast.

I slammed the door shut and pressed my body against it, not sure if the door could hold him, hollering the whole time. "I'm in here!" There are many ways God helps us and many times we have no idea that he is helping us.

When younger I didn't understand nor did I even contemplate how important God watching over me was; instead I took it for granted. But things began to change as I got older and I began to understand more fully how great his grace was.

While I had once thought that nobody would ever want to marry me, I did get married and had my first child, a daughter, when we lived in Patagonia, Arizona. It is very important to this story that Patagonia is described as it is a small, remote, rural town in southern Arizona over an hour away from any significant civilization. There were two restaurants and one hotel plus one church. I remember when we first moved there the first advice we were given was that there was no law in town as the different families in town fought often amongst themselves and so the law oftentimes shifted from family to family, making it basically non-existent.

It was a dark night and in Patagonia it got so dark that you couldn't see your hand in front of your face when the lights were out. Exacerbating this darkness, I couldn't see much of anything when I did not have my contacts in which I did not as I lay on the living room floor with my 6-month-old daughter, Teressa.

We had fallen asleep to the hum and flickering grey shadows of the TV. For no reason, about nine in the evening, both of us awoke at the same time. My daughter began fussing a little, so I thought a toy might amuse her. Getting up, I spied a dark object less than a foot from her head and bent over to pick it up as I imagined it could only be a toy.

I grew up in Montana. We don't tend to have a lot of bugs. I oftentimes thought it was probably because temperatures could plummet to forty below and sometimes summer only came for a month or two, not enough time for bugs to become too big or too populated. So, bugs were never a big concern for me which I appreciated it greatly as I never liked them much. And I had just moved to Arizona so I never thought about nor knew much about any of their bugs and such.

As I bent over to pick up the toy, a inner voice screamed in my head, "It's a scorpion! Grab your baby and run!" So insistent and fierce the scream was that I never hesitated. I grabbed my daughter and ran as fast as I could into my bedroom. Breathless from the fear, I yelled at my husband, "Don't ask me how I know, but I think there is a scorpion in the other room!"

Shortly, my husband returned. "Yep," he confirmed. "It was a scorpion. Made an awful vinegar smell when I squished it."

Checking the scorpion out now that it was dead and I was braver, we discovered it was a creamy colored small scorpion known as a bark scorpion. These are common in Arizona but also the deadliest especially for the most vulnerable being older people and young children, especially under the age of 2. If stung, it is critical that a young patient get medical care within the hour. We would never have made it if my daughter had been stung for the only hospital was two hours away in Tucson. To this day, I still thank God for the miracle that let my daughter live for she has brought me joy beyond anything I could ever have hoped for.

One thing I learned as a mother is that not only is our middle name "worry" as my mom always told me, but as a mother you need to pray incessantly. One thing a mom learns is that most things in the world are not in our control, especially as our children grow older and more independent. There were other times when I almost lost my daughters, but for the grace of God.

A few years later, we left Patagonia and moved to Tucson. We enjoyed family time together which included walks around the neighborhood. When my daughter got old enough, we got her one of those classic hot wheel cycles which she loved and drove fast. She would race her Cabbage patch hot wheels around the sidewalks, hugging the ground closely with us following as closely as we could after her. But as she got older, she got faster and faster.

Ours was a quiet neighborhood. Not many people coming and going as these were times when people didn't spend much time outdoors or with neighbors unlike when I grew up when streets were full of kids. It was a lovely evening with the Arizona evening warmth lulling us into complacency.

Suddenly, my daughter slammed on her brakes. I almost toppled over her and began to chastise her. At that moment, a large SUV vehicle backed up quickly down the driveway, less than a foot from where my daughter had stopped. I had not heard nor seen the vehicle so I am sure at her young age she had not either. I have always wondered why she stopped.

We didn't take so many walks anymore after that. To this day I still feel the dread of how close I came once again to losing my daughter which would have destroyed my life as I love her dearly.

CHAPTER 6  HOME SWEET HOME

Although miracles are enticing, the true genius and love of God is demonstrated in how he watches over even the most ordinary of us in the smallest of ways.

Several more years passed and I had a second daughter, Gemavie Marie.  Wanting to stay at home with my daughters, I was determined to find a job where I could work at home but in these times nobody worked at home as computers were not common nor was there an internet.  Still I tried, but everywhere I went I was abruptly turned down, barely able to say a word before being dismissed.

But I persevered for I believe you can't fail if you keep trying.  I had reached my limit though and thought about giving up. Exasperated, I had reached the point of giving up and was greatly saddened because I didn't want to leave my daughters for nothing in my life had given me more joy and I treasured every moment with them. Feeling desperate, I searched for something, anything, I could do to comfort myself. I perused the paper one more time which is where jobs at that time were most oftentimes listed. I saw an ad for an office assistant, read it carefully several times, but kept telling myself it was hopeless. Even after all of my experiences with the miraculous I still had not recognized that God watched over me.

I thought, "It will be the same as all of the others that said no. They won't let me work at home." Lost for possibilities, I looked at the ad one more time. To assuage myself, I decided to send a letter and resume, expecting nothing. How great is God who does not give up on us even when we do.

Within the week I got a phone call from the place in the ad requesting an interview. Having been turned down all the other times, I was trying hard during my drive to the interview to bolster my deflated and hopeless ego. To strengthen the possibility they would let me work at home, I kept practicing my argument over and over of how I would convince them of my plan, the same argument I had tried so many times before and failed as well as praying.

When I sat down for the interview, before I could say anything, the man conducting the interview said, "I need to tell first because you may not want the job but we would like you to work at home."

Being able to work at home was the greatest. I loved being home all the time with my daughters. One quiet morning when my oldest daughter was at grade school, I was working hard because I had a lot of work. My youngest daughter was playing quietly next to me when I got the most awful feeling, a feeling of pure evil.

The intensity of the inner voice in my head warning me of the evil was so compelling I began pacing around in the house as though I was confident I would find the source. I looked and looked, yet I could find nothing amiss.

Finding nothing in my house, I began looking up and down my street, over and over again but I saw nothing, nothing in my front yard, nothing anywhere else, but the sick uneasy feeling remained unabated. As I kept staring my eyes focused on the house across the street and as though my eyes were glued to it, I couldn't look away. I was mesmerized by it, but saw nothing. Still the inner voice inside of me kept insisting something was terribly wrong.

I knew the woman who owned the house across the street rented out rooms but knew nothing of who lived there with her. I wondered if I should call the cops but not sure what I would say other than I had a bad feeling which I didn't think they would take too seriously. But as I stood there with the minutes ticking by, I could see absolutely nothing, just the awful sick feeling in my gut. Finally, I reminded myself I had a pile of work waiting to be finished so I reluctantly returned to my office.

About 15 minutes later, my doorbell rang. I knew then it was connected to what was wrong. At my door stood a young girl, about 18 years old. She mumbled, "I rent a room across the street" and began apologizing profusely. "I am so sorry to have bothered you. I am being very silly. There really is no reason for me to be here."

"I know why you are here," I blurted out, urging her to come in. "Something is terribly wrong."

Stunned, she asked, "How do you know that?" The look on her face was more confused, but relieved as though she wondered if I could read her mind or knew something she did not.

Relieved, believing I believed her, she poured her story out. "As I was putting the key in the door I had an awful feeling. So awful scary enough that I felt I had to come over here. There is no reason why I should have been scared, I just was."

She finished, "Thinking about it, there really is nothing. I'm okay. Sorry again to have bothered you."

With no doubt in my mind anymore, I decisively told her, "You can't go over there" and she succumbed readily.

"We need to call the police," I demanded.

"What will we say?" she wondered. "I don't know that anything is wrong. I didn't see anything."

Although I had hesitated earlier to call the police, with her there I knew without question it had to be done although neither of us knew anything other than the awful feelings that unceasingly overwhelmed us.

"There is something bad happening in the house across the street from me," I told the 911 operator.

"What is your emergency," the 911 operator asked.

Reacting to our guts, we hadn't thought of what to say, but still we persisted. "I think something awful is happening the house across the street. Maybe someone broke in." The operator didn't seem to sense the awful urgency that we both felt.

I insisted, "You need to send someone as soon as possible."

"Yes, ma'am" the voice on the other end of the phone said nonchalantly, which was not reflective of the intense seriousness of my request. I wasn't so sure they would be coming, but we waited.

Still we waited and about an hour later the police did come. The young girl gave him her key and he went in.

"Who hates who?" he asked when he finally came out about 15 minutes later. He continued, "That house is a mess. They did weird things in there, like to the crucifixes, cutting up everything, destroying and breaking things, and much more." He asked why we had called, and we told him it was just a feeling. "Well," he said, "it's wise to listen to your feelings." I didn't want to tell him it was the inner voice in my head talking to me.

Shaken and sickened contemplating what might have happened to her if she had gone in, the young girl asked, "What would have happened to me?"

"You must have disturbed them in the middle of cutting everything up with knives because they left in the middle of doing that when they heard you at the door," he replied, "If you had gone in then you would walked right into the kitchen where they were. No telling what would have happened to you. Somebody saved your life today."

We learned later that not only was the young girl's life spared but the house as well as there were other similar break-ins in the neighborhood where ultimately they burned the house down.

This event, as well as many others, reminded me constantly of how precious a gift my daughters were. Though I worked hard my whole life, just like my mom did, I never had much money so we went without most things. Sometimes this caused problems with my daughters because they wondered why they couldn't have the things that everyone else had. As gracious as they are though, they were easily made happy when we got dollar kids meals at Grandy's Chicken. Most importantly though, despite having no money, we made great memories together forever.

While in grade school, a sacrifice I made for my daughters were piano lessons. My oldest had become quite proficient and when she was in the sixth grade her music teacher asked her to play a song at one of the school's church services.

Thrilled, I of course accepted readily for her though I knew little about pianos. Afterwards I realized her little keyboard which was less than half the size of keys of a regular piano did not provide her the opportunity to practice properly to play a life-size piano. Uncertain and concerned that my daughter would not have experience to play on a full piano, I talked with the music teacher who offered to let her practice in the school's music room.

Feeling guilty, I bowed my head in prayer, as I sat listening to her practicing. I had worked hard my whole life, I had tried so hard, and she had worked so hard too, but I knew there was no way I could ever afford a real piano for her. These are the kinds of things, especially when you feel that you are holding your children back, that a parent feels they have failed their children, as I did now.

As she played, I poured my discouragement and guilt out onto God. "I feel so bad I have no way to buy her a real piano," I prayed. Engrossed in my sorrowful prayer, I didn't hear someone enter the room. It was the janitor, Joe. I had talked many times with him before and he was a very kind person who would help anyone.

"She's great! I thought she was the music teacher!" he exclaimed.

He lifted my spirits as he always did. Smiling back at him, I murmured, "Thank you."

With that, he left, and I returned to my prayers of woe.

Within a few minutes, he returned. Hollering from the door, he cried out, "Do you want a piano?"

Dumbfounded, the only response I could utter was "Sure."

Unbelieving, I watched as the door closed after him again. "Oh well," I thought. "Maybe he felt my sadness and wanted to cheer me up." Sad as I was, I didn't believe he meant that he would get me a piano, so I went back to woefully praying.

Returning ten minutes later, he explained, "Have someone here on Friday to pick it up."

I wasn't sure what he meant. I wasn't sure if he really meant what I thought he had just said. I wasn't sure how to respond. I knew he couldn't really be referring to a piano, but I didn't know.

"What do you mean?" I asked him.

"Someone needs to be here on Friday to pick up the piano to take to your house," he finished.

"Okay," I thought. "I can go along with this ruse. Maybe there was some misunderstanding." Quickly he scurried off, leaving me more confused than ever.

I thought about it for days, wondering if I should arrange for someone to go to the church to pick the piano up though I was certain there would be no piano.

"But what if, what if, there really was a piano?" I wondered. "Can't hurt to have someone go there. Then when there is nothing, at least I tried." Sometimes I just never gave up, especially with hope. I was also used to being disappointed in my life, so I thought, "I just won't get my hopes up because then I won't be disappointed, something I am quite familiar with. No one gives pianos away."

I must digress in my story at this point to add an important element. Every night for well over a year before my daughters and I said our prayers, When my youngest daughter would pray for a grand piano, I thought every time I should explain to her such things don't happen, but it was so sweet to see her faith and hope that nothing is impossible with God.?

On Friday I waited, not expecting anyone to show. But around noon there was a knock on the door and there was a piano. But not just a piano, a grand piano!

As explained to me later, someone had donated a newer grand piano to the church and so they were willing to give me the piano. To this day the grand piano sits in my dining room, taking up pretty much the whole room. I think I am stuck with it forever for how do you give away such a great blessing from God?

One thing I have learned with God is don't try to make deals as he always wins. I always loved helping others and have been greatly blessed in being able to make miracles happen in the most hopeless of lives. Though I didn't have magic, God is able to make miracles happen and oftentimes he expects us to be the ones to make good things happen for others.

Having a love for helping others, I have volunteered extensively in my life for all kinds of people and agencies. This was also true of my daughters' school where I volunteered for anything and everything. Being there always gave me the opportunity to know that things were well and I could get to know the teachers and staff well.

At the school I helped with everything from health clinics to Christmas fairs and fiestas as well as the classrooms and even as a board member. An easy going person, I always helped anyone or anywhere, staying out of any drama or conflict that threatened to destroy the good that I had wanted to do, but sometimes it can be difficult to avoid.

Things are almost always never what we thought they were. Assumptions are a deadly affair, destroying without knowing. Though the things of our world today are not the most important things oftentimes they seem so important but later we realize they never were. But something seemed very important to a particular mom one day during a barbecue I had organized for the students. She began yelling at me and for many months after avoided me or scowled at me.

A couple of years passed and one day, for no reason at all, the inner voice began telling me I should visit her. "Visit her," I thought. "Really, so she can yell at me more! I highly doubt that she wants me to visit her. Besides I have no idea how to get a hold of her." So I ignored the inner voice.

Still it persisted. "Darn," I thought, feeling guilty, but wishing it would go away because I did not want to do what it was telling me."

So I reasoned. "Since I don't know how to get a hold of her, I certainly can't see her. I'll try calling the school but I know they won't give me any information because they can't give out numbers." Truly, I did not know how to get a hold of her otherwise.

"She is in the hospital," they confided. That only intensified the arguments of the inner voice.

So I made a deal with God. "If I can't find someone to go the hospital with me," I proposed, "then I won't go." I tried to sabotage it by stating I had to only call one person and if that one person can't go, then I don't have to."

I tried to think of someone who might be home as I figured I had to put some legitimate effort into the whole thing but someone who is always too busy to do anything else, especially at the last moment. I dialed the phone of one of my friends thinking she would not even answer the phone.

"Hello," I heard. It was one of those moments when you wish you wouldn't have to talk to or see some particular person though this time was not because I didn't like my friend but rather I had lost the deal. I remained confident though that she would be too busy.

"Eileen, can you go to the hospital with me? I just found out that this mom is there and I just thought maybe I should go visit her."

Sure of her "no," I was surprised with her quick "yes" followed by "I'll be right over," condemning me to do something I really did not want to go and seeing someone I had avoided for a long time after our last nasty encounter several years before.

Oh how I was dreading this. "Why I hadn't just forgotten the whole thing" and "how dumb my deal-making had been" were my regrets. There really was no reason whatsoever why I should visit her. I couldn't understand why I should have to visit someone who didn't like me at all as evidenced by her past tirade at me. And I certainly shouldn't be upsetting her at the hospital because the last thing a sick person needs is the one person they hated. But the time for arguments was over and the deal sealed.

A short time later, my friend and I headed off to the hospital. I couldn't think of anything I should say to the mom when I got there, so my mind remained blank when I walked into her room. I felt like a fool walking into her room, certain she would scream at me all over again, sure that I could only make things worse for her in the hospital.

I was shocked at her words. "You are the one person I've been praying to see!" she exclaimed. Humbled by her tears and exclamation of joy at seeing me, I stood there saying nothing.

"I was so awful to you and treated you so horrible," she continued. "You were always so nice to me. I should never have treated you so bad. I have wanted for a long time to tell you how sorry I was. It was around that time that I began getting sick though."

With a serious dose of humbleness, I felt gratefully thankful I had not returned her anger with anger long ago and that I had obeyed the inner voice.

"I had fought the cancer for several years but now I am told I have little time left, but still always I wanted to tell you I was sorry," she finished. I was speechless because of the many horrible things people did to me throughout my life what she did was not that bad. I was deeply impressed because in her worst of times she was concerned about how I felt and wanted to apologize, something that the others who hurt me never had done.

That night she passed away.

## CHAPTER 8  CARS AND PLANES

"Darn," I thought. "Late again. Gotta speed up!"  It was a late afternoon several years later and I had just gotten off of work. I was already late to my daughter's volleyball game.  Being a single parent, I always wanted to be there, everywhere, for my daughters. I looked down the long straight road with little traffic heading in my direction, so I stepped on the gas.

Pima was a four lane road in Tucson, with two lanes in each direction.  I was headed west when I noticed I was going below the speed limit. Being already late, I continued to speed up.  As quickly as I contemplated speeding up, the inner voice in my head began fervently ordering me to slow down.  I still wasn't the best at complying with the inner voice so I began arguing with it instead.

As much I tried to ignore the inner voice, it only grew more intense. Checking the traffic in both directions, I argued, "There is no one going my way," although far ahead I could see the traffic in the opposite direction headed east was stopped.

Still the inner voice adamantly continued, "You need to slow down." However, still I didn't listen and kept going faster. As I got closer I could see that a mangy yellow-colored mutt was blocking the opposite lanes, walking slowly off the road on their side.

Believing there was no good reason why I should slow down, I kept increasing my speed. Sill the inner voice insisted I slow down, and still I argued with it.

"You know, the dog could change directions and come back into your lane," the inner voice argued.

"But it's almost off the road on the other side," I countered.

As the constancy and intensity of the inner voice's arguments continued, I finally relented and began slowing down.

Yet still the inner voice continued unabated, saying I should slow down even more. I was done arguing so without hesitation I slowed even more.

When I was right before where the dog was crossing, he did turn around and started walking into my lanes. Thankful, I sighed. I loved dogs and hurting one would have been emotionally very difficult for me.

I slammed on my brakes to stop completely to avoid the dog which thankfully I could do because I was going so slow.

Just then a baby in diapers stepped out of the bushes on the side and into the lane in front of me!

I flung my car door open, jumping out in a second, abandoning my car with no thought of its safety or mine for the lane next to me was open and a car could come along any time.   I grabbed the baby and ran into the trailer park on the side of the road. Hearing voices coming from one of the trailers, I called out and a mom came running out.  "My baby, my baby!" she hollered.

"Lady," I breathlessly told her, "if it wasn't for your mutt, your baby would be dead.  Your mutt stopped all of the traffic."

Turning the whitest shade of pale, the mom muttered, "It's not my mutt.  It's a stray that wandered into our trailer park today and I was going to take it to the dog pound but hadn't been able to get there yet."

Cars are one of the most dangerous and deadliest possessions. I've had a lifetime of troubles with cars.  I am certain that as a single female I was oftentimes the prey of some unscrupulous people because I have had to replace transmissions and engines on cars with only 50,000 miles on them.  But my lifetime of car troubles taught me many things about taking care of cars.

It was Saturday morning and I had dropped my young daughters off at their dance class. Even though I had a regular mechanic, my brakes were squeaking so I thought I'll just take the car to Brakemasters because getting new brakes is not a big deal and this way I wouldn't have to miss work during the week to get them repaired.

There were several people in the lobby waiting for their cars at Brakemasters. Most were guys and one young girl. Quickly and easily, Brakemasters were able to assist the men at a reasonable cost, usually under $100. I sighed relief for I thought I had at least found an honest reasonable place.

More men came and went, and still the young girl and I sat and waited. Now I was starting to get worried.

My deep dread was realized when the mechanic entered and told the young girl she needed a lot of work done on her brakes and it would cost about $600. I knew this meant things were not going to go well at all. She said she couldn't afford it and would have to talk to her dad and left. Now I alone waited, dreading the awful outcome which I was sure would come now.

Wondering if there was any hope where I could grab my car and run, the mechanic returned. "You need $1000.00 in repairs. Some serious problems that need to be taken care of right away. We wouldn't even want you to drive with brake like that."

I responded, "Put my wheels back on." I thought, "I'll take it to my mechanic on Monday."

Still, I waited. "What could take so long now?" I wondered. But eventually they did bring my car around to the front. Saddened by their deviousness, I left.

I picked my daughters up from their class and headed home, going 60 mph down a freeway. Suddenly the car began shaking back and forth violently. It was terrifying. I had never seen or ever heard of a car shaking so violently.

Somehow I managed to pull the car off the freeway and limp into a tire shop that was closing. A young mother with two small children, I begged them, "Please. "Please look at my tires! Something is terribly wrong!"

They relented. I think sometimes in this life we forget how important good people are and how much we depend on their kindness. Instead in our world too often we don't appreciate good people and take them for granted, but I did not take these guys for granted and many years later I am still thankful for them.

After a short time, they came out shaking their heads. "None of the lug nuts were tightened on your car, all four tires were ready to fall off at any time. I don't know how you made it here! Someone was watching over you."

CHAPTER 5 FINALE

Although it has been a long journey for me, everything in the world, and in particular my own experiences, have demonstrated clearly that there is a personal God who loves us, personal because he does care about every one of us, sometimes in the smallest, most personal, ways. What I did learn was you have to let him be a part of your life rather than thinking you are wiser and greater so you don't need him for truly it is a wise person who realizes they don't know much at all, and I have certainly learned that in my life.

It is incredible and ludicrously hypocritical when people tell me they can't believe in God because he can't be seen anywhere and he does nothing for them, especially not fixing the consequences of their bad choices. If we cannot hear or know him it is because we have chosen to close our eyes and ears to him. I spent a lifetime learning to listen and know God.

While I have told some of the stories in my life of how great and good God is to us, there are many more. Some of the most important lessons I learned through it all is that what I wanted was not the best, in fact, none of what I thought I wanted was good for me. I am glad God didn't listen to me when I whined about my need for the things of the world. I have discovered over time that the things of the world I thought I wanted were terrible in fact and would have created a miserable life for me. I am eternally grateful to God who gave me gifts that far exceeded the joy and successed I had ever hoped for.

While many other religions and philosophies believe people can't change, Christianity believes there is always hope for everyone no matter how hopeless or hurt. Though I thought I was less than ordinary, hopeless and alone, God never gave up on me and blessed me with extraordinary miracles.

IT IS AN EVIL GENERATION THAT DEMANDS A MIRACLE TO BELIEVE (MATTHEW 12:39)

www.ingramcontent.com/pod-product-compliance
Lightning Source LLC
Chambersburg PA
CBHW060717030426
42337CB00017B/2911